Table of Contents

Jamie
05/2016

Passive-Aggressive

It's okay if you don't want to read this poem.
Really,
It's no big deal.

And yes,
I swear I wrote this one-
that it's not another test
like that time I showed you two poems
and told you they were both mine,
but one was by a famous poet.

When you chose mine as the better of the two,
I said it only went to show
you knew nothing about poetry.

But this isn't like that-
I promise.
And besides, you've probably got something better to do
than read a silly poem that's about you.

So I guess you'll miss the part
where I write something really small
                I love you!
and when you lean down to read it,
the poem grabs your nose
and squeezes so hard your eyes start to water-
which is good
because the sad part is coming.

The part about how much I miss you.

But yeah, I know,
you're tired
and all I do is talk about poetry.
Poetry this and poetry that,
blah blah blah.

All you had to do was read the stupid thing,
then say thank you
for the tan you got
while basking in its brilliance.

It doesn't matter anyway
because the poem's over now
and I'm going to kill myself.
Thanks.
Thanks a lot.

Still Life with Jacket

I can still smell my father
in the morning
when the client's backyard is thick
with pines and sparrows.

I become a child camping
with meals-ready-to-eat,
the packet of mashed potatoes
looking more like milk
than anything potato-like
and my father laughing, saying,
"Don't tell your mother."

Or my father drunk and getting a ticket
for not wearing a life-jacket
on his hand-made fishing boat
and later grumbling around the campfire
about how nobody's allowed to be a man anymore.

And now that grumble is in me,
on mornings like these,
when the houses I'm painting
become jackets
I'll never take off.

Bacon

You cure of hangover,
friend of the simple hash brown
that I am.

Cover your tender pink ears
when the miserable healthy
speak to you of carcinogens
and cholesterol.

They can no longer smell
your muggy perfume,
nor taste
your sometimes brittle beauty.

I alone will be faithful to you
my sizzling little mistress,
my porcine goddess.

I alone
am willing to die for you.

Eat the Rich: A Recipe

Preheat the oven to 451 degrees,
the temperature at which money burns.

Next, take three SUV's,
crack them in two
and remove the whites.

Then mix together in a bowl
with two self-satisfied peels of laughter
from a soccer mom.

Bake for a generation.

Garnishing options:

Diced Debutante
Julienned CEO
Dash of Trustafarian
Ladle of Landlord

Fantasy Rejection Letter

Dear Esteemed Author,

I apologize for the stains
on the returned ms.

It appears that your characters
were so round, so fresh and ripe,

that when turning the page
they burst right open,
ruining any subsequent reading on our part.

Please send us another copy
and we shall proceed with the appropriate care.

Most humbly,

The Editors

There It Is

I'm standing in our backyard
and God help me
the sky is filled with cotton
and the cigarette smoke is more cotton
and all I can think of are varicose veins
the way the blue split the clouds
along your thighs and the moon
is just another eye
and all I want is to make this life matter
but I feel so ridiculously significant
exactly when I shouldn't
and I know how silly it is
to be talking about the moon
factual or otherwise
but there it is
and I'm sad because you are no longer here
and I chose to stay
and the last thing I wanted to do was write about this
but there it is…our death
hanging right above us
where the stars used to be.

Two Figures of Speech Walk into a Bar

Simile: I'll have, um, like a beer.

Bartender: You got it. How about your friend here?

Metaphor: I'll have a warm hand massaging my soul.

Bartender: I don't think we have that.

Simile: I'm sorry. He'll have, um, like a whiskey.

Rat Commits Mutiny

In the morning,
I found you hanging
by the pink
of your knotted tail.

What order did you refuse?
Or were you like me
and simply born with petulant whiskers?

Did you see your death
scurrying towards you
from the horizon?

When the noose took its hold
did you row your arms
toward a landlocked heaven?

It was me, the boatswain,
who cut you down
and slungshot you out to sea
among the waves crumbling
like so much Feta cheese.

Writer's Almanac

I want to hear my poem
dipped in NyQuil,
sleepwalking out the radio
from atop my forty-foot ladder.

I want to hear you nasal out the words
'The poet, Jamie Zerndt.'
How absurd and ridiculous
that would sound.

But instead, at 10:06 am,
you leave me with those three cuds of Midwestern solace
not even a Woebegonian cow would chew on:

Be Well
Do Good Work
and Keep in Touch.

Rockefellered

There are nights like these
lying in our backyard
choking on hiccups
as the dog wonders about the state
of moonlight and I try to explain
how the universe conspired
yet again
to get me drunk
but he looks suspicious
so I write poems
and hand them to him
one after another
like blank checks
from a broke philanthropist.

People-ing

I told you that sometimes fish go people-ing.

You looked up at me
then at the little mouths
poking holes in the algae.

Your smile began to quiver
and slowly-
you stepped away from the bank.

Buddha Explains To The Flight Attendant Why There's Part Of A Haiku On His Lap

Only enough room
to stuff fourteen syllables
in the overhead

How to Raise an American Artist

Break her legs at birth
and every time thereafter
when she shows any interest
in sports.

Change her last name
to 'Zilla' so she sits
in the back row for life.

Make her Ivy-intolerant
so she pukes
upon hearing the word 'Harvard.'

Name her 'God'
to instill wrath
and let the attack on New York begin.

Wisconsin Mourning

The lake's been electrocuted again.
the mist sizzling
from its bald surface,
the fish all capsizing
while the loons keen.

Soon the cicadas, too,
will throw their voices
across the water
in protest.

I can almost remember how all this used to look,
back before you left us,
back before sentence was passed
on all the good things.

Your Death Sits By The Window

watching a cloud

lodged like a piece of lint

in the belly of the sky

while somewhere around the corner

there's the sound of a lawnmower

hitting a rock—

a run-on sentence

finding its period

buried in the grass.

Then the importuning silence

causing death to open its mouth

as if maybe an old lover has called out

its name.

The Ocean Took a Vacation

She thought she might be bi-polar,
but the doctors prescribed Dramamine
and a visit to the city where she could spend time
gazing at a horizon of skyscrapers.

She brought the moon along,
took his picture posing
beside the rows of street lights.
The two collected beer cans
to bring home and place upon her shelf of sand.

But when she returned home,
the fishing boats felt her tossing
in her sleep again.

As she paced her floor in the morning,
it wasn't the medication,
or the kelp-tea,
that made it possible for her to return to work.

It was placing the shell
of an empty can of PBR to her ear,
listening to the distant roar of car alarms,
and remembering the boyfriend-lit strolls at midnight,
that eventually returned her sea-legs to her.

Not Thinking

I'm not thinking about the odds
involved in watching my father die
while visiting for the first time in years.

Not thinking about the bathroom, the bile
I can still smell on my fingers, as I drive
away from him.

I'm not thinking
about being unable to lift him
from the toilet
or about telling my mother again that
yes, I'm sure,
he's dead.

Instead, I think about what I see:

the old men atop John Deere tractors
waving in plaid shirts
like easy stalks of wheat,

the retreads from trucks
and jaywalking deer
shredded along the roadside,

the dogged mountains
with their fir trees
shaved away after surgery,

the cows
looking like burnt-out logs
lying at the bottom
of the plain's fire pit,

the old barns drunk
and draping their shadows
over the landscape,

the small towns
who place giant letters
made from white rocks
on the face of their biggest hill
like so many distress signals.

Did You Paint This?

He's seen the painting before,
been to my place before,
tripped his finger along the spines of my books
like a stick along a fence,
but tonight it's "snowing"
as he likes to say,
and suddenly the painting has begun to glow
right along with us.

Which is funny
because there is snow in the painting
and a dog standing in the corner
next to an old house.

He tells me he'd really like to buy the painting
if only I'd consider changing this one thing.
When I tell him I like it the way it is,
I can tell he thinks he's stumbled upon a real artist.

We go on getting impressed with one another,
the two of us chewing on our teeth
long into the night,
but in the morning my throat feels like a blowtorch
and my date is nowhere to be found.

The painting, though, is still there,
my name along the bottom
steaming and yellowing
as if the dog, under cover of night,
had decided to autograph the snow.

She's a Real Pistil

I've never been good with names.

Like this flower
with its orange house and yellow trim
or the fly inside it
wearing a phosphorescent purple zoot suit
and yellow tap shoes
dancing around six slender sisters
as they stand in a circle
all with identical hats.

I watch as he picks one out
and starts humping her
right there in the living room
while all the neighbors
turn up their television sets
to drown out the cries of pleasure.

Rental Agreement

I fell in love with my hangover
and we've decided to move in together.

It was time:
either this was something we were serious about,
or we needed to go our separate ways.

She says her room must be padded with fog,
that the walls will sweat whenever she moves.

There are two cats coming as well--
Resolution and Thirst.
Who, she says, will never get along,
but need one another just the same.

Then there's the smell
of empty suitcases
threatening to fill up,

but I'm not worried:
she promises never to be around
at night.

First Poetry Reading

They all do it
in the same
ca-
dence.

I discover that night
a kind of DNA to poetry-
something that makes the words climb up
and down a ladder,
their feet pausing
where the rungs twist
with irony.

Afterwards I sit in a restaurant,
pick up a menu, and, in my best
Captain Kirk voice,
give my first reading to an audience
of silverware:

Meatballs
with Parmesan
and Egg
Plant
drenched in a hearty
red sauce
Seven
Nine-
ty
Nine.

House Painting

The back of the house stands there half-naked
with whatever clothes she does have on
hanging in tatters.

When she sees me coming toward her,
glinting steel in hand,
she plays hard to get.

We go at it all day, though,
until finally she strips bare
and I leave her there,
spent,
dreaming of the Black Plum dress
I've promised to buy her.

Apology

My grandfather used to take his boat out
into the middle of the lake
and play his acoustic guitar.

Out came these wrinkled blues
cast over the water like an apology
to all the fish he'd ever killed.

When he finished,
we'd listen to the wake
clapping hard
against the dock.

Buddha Complex

I am a lotus
thumper.

I have belly
envy.

I am the sound
of one ego clapping.

War Criminal

"For many years, we have enjoyed the convenience of killing bugs
with aerosols."
-*taken from a can of Poison-Free Wasp & Hornet Killer*

I killed the whole family,
squashed their collective womb
into the shingles
before kicking it off the roof,
their honeycombed home
left in a puddle of mint-scented, poison-free poison.

If I were caught and interrogated
they'd think I was lying
when I told them I didn't know
the difference between a hornet and a wasp,
that none of it was racially motivated.

I can still see one cursiving around
the hole where her future used to be,
spelling out the word
m-u-r-d-e-r-e-r
over and over.

I hope she took some satisfaction
in watching as I tripped down the ladder,
a frightened dictator
fearing a tribunal of stings.

Felony Flats

At one in the morning the wind is camouflaged
in old newspapers and car exhaust
as fifteen men circle two
in the strip-club parking lot
across from my rented house.

It's like a hip-hop version of West Side Story,
the words *No lead, no steal!* being shouted over and over
as the traffic lights swing like lanterns
and the fast food wrappers
tumble-weed by.

But I'm safe inside
as I listen to the police sirens signaling the denouement
and I imagine them all breaking into song,
Maria bursting from the strip-club doors,
her face angelic, too pure for the dirt
of Felony Flats.

I think of going outside,
warning whoever's playing the part of Tony
not to run to her,
that he isn't going to make it,
that Maria's going to end up addicted to Meth,
that she's going to leave him for the producer.

But it's too late,
the gun's already gone off.

Antiques Road Show

Do you see here,
the generous play of light?
That was our first clue
that we might be on to something of value.

And when I saw the signature, here,
my heart sped up.

But, unfortunately, you see,
it really is quite worthless.
What did you pay?
Five dollars?
Well, let's just say you tipped the vendor well.

It has all the qualities,
at first glance,
of a world-class poem.
But once you hold it up to the light,
you begin to see the words
are all over-polished.

Note the patina here: artificial.

Even the similes
have all been rubbed down
to nothing.

Floyd's Coffee

They converted the old gas station
into a drive-thru coffee shop.
Before the black-haired girl
leans her tattooed arm out the window
like a sultry gas nozzle
to fill the cars up with espresso
I have to drive over a long black hose
that looks like a snake
only it makes this "ding-ding" sound
instead of a *hiss*.
And every morning before work
I line up with the rest
and watch this poor old hose
being dragged from his coiled retirement
just when he probably thought
his days of being stepped on
were finally over.

The Party

The earth is a piñata
stuffed with death certificates
while all the various gods circle round
waiting to swing bats
at what they jokingly refer to
as candy.

Reasons Why the World Should Have Stopped

For telling me
over and over again
that Hemingway was a fraud-
though I think you loved him more than anyone.

For drinking Manhattans
after visiting the doctor's office
and declaring with a grand toast,
"What do they know?"

For writing a letter to Gillette
and telling them you were ashamed of them-
that just because a razor had three blades
didn't make the quality of the shave any better.

For having only eight people at your funeral,
a feat that somehow rivals the crowds
of lesser men and women.

For dying poor,
your outdated
Willy-Loman virtue
still perfectly
intact.

Coroner

My father has been dead now
for 64 minutes
and I'm here
holding my mother's hand,
as dead, almost, as his
and you want to know
"the details."

You tell me it's called aspiration
when I pressed my mouth to my father's,
our first kiss in twenty-five years,
and found a lake of bile
pouring back into me.

I hear something about a possible autopsy,
something more about not worrying,
that it shouldn't be necessary
since, after all, he was 78,
but first you have to make a phone call
and "make sure."

You don't notice my mother's hand
squeezing mine,
don't sense how desperately I wish
it was wrapped around
your still-breathing throat.

The Moon was Taking Pictures of Her Again

and I got jealous,
marched right up there,
picked his pocket,
asked what the meaning was
of all those snapshots in his wallet.

I yelled into his lye-pocked face:
"I see how she looks at you,
but she's mine,
so stop peering through our window!"

He mumbled something about how nobody
paid any attention to him anymore,
something about how he used to be
a white mirror
reflecting multitudes of wonder.

Honestly, I've never understood
what all the fuss was about the moon.
I mean I wasn't going to sit there
and coddle his waning ego
if that's what he was after.

"You're just a big old bully
pushing around the ocean.
An albino pancake,
an over-rated spit-ball,
a yellowing hangnail,
a doorknob to nothing,
a glory-hole for Sunday poets."

He didn't say anything,
just dropped his head
and proceeded to make
the slowest
escape
ever.

Bullshit Villanelle

We were asked to choose two lines and execute a style.
It was poetic benevolence because somewhere in Iraq,
A woman was smelling a foul odor, noticing a pile.

The newspaper talked about the stack of Iraqi dead, while
we sipped our coffee and practiced how to care.
We were asked to choose two lines and execute a style.

I tried to be clever and put the men on trial
but absurdity has a stench, too, so beware
the woman smelling a foul odor, noticing a pile.

I buckled down like all the rest, tried not to smile.
If asked to read one aloud, who would dare?
We were asked to choose two lines and execute a style.

We poets understood her pain, went the extra mile
to give metaphorical light to her husband's dead stare
while she was smelling a foul odor, noticing a pile.

I titled mine *How to Find Poetic Fodder in War*
but hung my head when asked to share.
We were asked to choose two lines and execute a style.
But I smelled a foul odor, noticed a different sort of pile.

House Painting Rain Delay

While sleeping,
my hand stiffens into a fist
clasped around an imaginary scraper.

It seems to hear the rain
and realizing it won't be forced to peel
the clothing from the world's most chaste woman,
relaxes and lets itself un-curl a little,
as if trying to shake hands with the rain,
as if to say:

Thank you.
Keep up the good work.

Black Out

A stranger leaves notes for me almost every night now.
I've never met him,
or her,
but their handwriting is erratic,
like a starving person's last words to the world.

I find them on the coffee table,
in the bathroom, in the backyard
with cigarette burns through their dry, crumpled skins.

I place them into a folder labeled
Return to Sender
just in case I ever run into
the poor delusional fool.

Snow Globe

A house sits alone on a hill,
leaning on a crutch,
groggy from pain meds.

Inside, an old woman
with young black hair
hunches over a sink
in frozen genuflection,
a dish held in her hands
like a single bead in a rosary.

In the living room, a bald head
leaves a patina on the leather couch.
Both the couch and the man are sagging,
dying one Manhattan,
one re-run at a time.

When I shake it,
the snow remains
like a dead halo
around the house.

I've been trying for years now,
but nothing ever moves,
nothing ever changes.

Into the Wild Blue Yonder

When you were done eating
our cue to leave a restaurant
was a long sigh
and an irritated cough.

How appropriate that after the funeral
while I was trying to figure out the name
of the old war song chiming away outside the church
your hearse backfired
before pulling away.

Wife Marooned in Bathwater

Her belly is an island
while inside
a child engineer
launches missiles
made of elbows and feet
warring for the simple right
to drown
like all the rest of us.

Stained Glass

There is love between what is broken
and what will be made whole again.

Her glass-cutter skates over colored ice
toward the table's edge,
forcing whole continents
to crack and splinter to the floor.

Scarred hands wave a hot wand
over the contours of a winter town
and if you follow the horseshoe nails
along the channels,
you will see the sole resident of the town,
frightened and unsure of its future,
crouching in the fields just below the sunset:

Light.

The Heroine of 7th Grade Science

I had a crush on you back then
because of a line
I saw scrawled on your notebook:
I eat dust.

Those three words made me put away the comic books,
say goodbye to Wolverine and hello to grizzly Bukowski
who used his words like steel blades.

And the first time you said Dostoyevsky's name,
it sounded both smooth and bumpy,
like how I imagined the cobbled streets of St. Petersburg to be.

Those books I read are still piled up inside of me,
their names waiting to be spoken so they won't disappear.

It was you, my dust-eating tom-boy,
who I'd fall in love with
again and again,
reincarnated in every girlfriend I'd ever have.

It was you who started this whole mess.

Looking for a Nail

The Gerber baby food jars with their lids
nailed to the underside of the shelf
are filled with the miscellaneous nuts and bolts
of a childhood.

They hover there in the garage,
and in my memory,
held by the simple genius of a father.

Ice

Your last breaths waltz across the ice
as it breaks beneath you
and the ice is a veil
a melting,
something waiting to absorb you
once again
and each breath is a rope cast
back to a land
I'm still standing on.

I know you are slipping into the black water
because I can see you
trying to convince yourself
this cold is your new home.

But then another rope is thrown
and the struggle begins anew.

There is a thawing inside of all of us,
a slow and constant disappearing.
Pray to what is melting
and hope it prays back.

The Snow A Procession Of Mourners

And what's the point of getting a poem
published in *The New Yorker*
now that you are gone
and won't be able to tell me
how you couldn't find a copy in all of Mercer
or Ironwood and had to drive all the way to Minocqua
and when you checked out you couldn't help but point out my name
to the woman behind the counter and tell her the name
is your son
and she smiles at you (but not long enough)
and you are so proud, so proud that you go back the next day
and buy another copy just so you can tell another person
that this is your son's poem and it's in *The New Yorker?*

But now it will just be a name there at the bottom
(Or do they put it at the top? I haven't bought a copy in years)
that means nothing to anybody
and gone now are the days when I can get drunk
and tell you how poetry is dying
that I suspect there is a factory somewhere—*A Poetry Factory*—
but that I can't find it and that most poetry is in love with itself
which is never really all that attractive
and when I mumble the lyrics to "Hang The DJ"
you'll ask me what I'm talking about
and care
and I'll tell you all about Morrissey and all the songs
on the radio never saying anything about his life
our lives
and we'll never get back around to the death of poetry
we'll forget what we were talking about and laugh
because we aren't all that bright sometimes
and then it'll take you three times to say goodbye like it always does
and I won't get irritated with you even once
and we'll talk about Dad and how we miss him still
how neither of us will ever forget that night
how I can't believe you can't remember all those towels
filled with bile that I threw in a Hefty bag

and drove to the dump the next day
so you wouldn't try washing them
like I knew you would.

The Smoke Stacks Of Longview's Paper Mills

wave like sock puppets
in the early morning light
as the welders at the community college
in mustard-yellow robes
bend to the day
looking like Trappist monks
in safety goggles
just in case enlightenment
comes searing through.

I Want To Write Something About The Airport

and how it keeps coming back to me,
how I'll be having a perfectly average day,
and there it will be, this image, memory, of you at Portland
International Airport...

You're wearing that old blue puffy Midwestern probably bought at
K-Mart coat of yours and you look full, a little heavy, but so healthy
and you're trying to give me some money before getting into the
security-check line and the money thing is always a source of
argument between us because I tell you not to do it but this time I
take it and say thank you because I'm out of work and I need it. I
don't take all of it, though, and stuff some back into your hand (Did
you ever find the check I snuck into your book? I wrote it before we
went to the airport because I knew you would try it again and this
time I would take the money all benevolent-like knowing you'd find
the check later. Did that ever really happen? Everything seems
suspect these days. I won't remember writing any of this later. I can
guarantee you that.) Anyway, I hope that didn't make you angry
when you found it. But what I do remember is the hug, the way you
really hugged me when we said goodbye. We would spend days
together and never reach that level of intimacy—but there, in front of
strangers, I could feel you holding onto me and me squeezing you
back, how fragile you seemed to me, how needy, how unlike I
normally saw you. I know you didn't want to leave. I know it. And I
stood there watching you go through the line, that funny little dance
you do when you go through the metal detector and the look you
would give the guy or gal as they scanned your body—like *I'm just a
harmless old lady, are you kidding me?* And that's how I'm
remembering you now, rather than as the emaciated, skinny finally,
on your death bed Mom—that pile of bills on the kitchen table you
were forever going to clean up no longer a worry—that's where you
are most days now, in an airport, forever receding, with me stuck
behind a barrier of some kind, a red rope of some kind, watching
with tears I'm glad you can't see.

I'd Be the Worst Kind of Famous

I'd walk like a diseased king
down busy streets
taking in the applause of car horns.

So self-engrossed would my ego be
that if a bird were to relieve himself on me
I'd think it a compliment:
a sure sign he could spot greatness
and was only trying to touch it
however vicariously.

Somebody, somewhere, must know all this-
which is why there's no mail today
and you forgot to call me back.

Among The Stacks

Every day at approximately the same time
a young Nick Drake wraiths among the stacks
and pulls the same book off the shelf only to return it
an hour later. And every day I vow to get up
after he leaves and see what book he keeps coming back to
because I want something like that, something to search for
and find, something to borrow and gently return again,
something like a secret I hope to be told again tomorrow
because I'm dying in here, grading papers on the upper floor
of a library, adding and crossing out commas like it really matters
when I could care less about commas or whether abortion is right
or wrong, or whether or not this particular student scores the winning
goal in their soccer match or if they did or didn't trip while walking
across the stage at their high school graduation or if their pig won
the blue ribbon because I want to read this Nick-Drake kid's essay
about how light he is, how he's able to float into libraries, how he's
only going to read this one book for the rest of his life because this
one book is magic, this one book has it all, this book has no commas,
no ideas about euthanasia or being abused as a child, this book has
no dead parents, no brother dying in a war nobody ever really cared
about in the first place.

I Spoke About You Today To My English Class

God they are so young, so blank and beautiful sitting there.
I referred to you only as "someone very close to me"
and that made it a little easier. I knew if I had said your name
I wouldn't be able to do it. I couldn't say *My mom died of cancer
a few months ago.* I just couldn't.

I can still see your clutched fist,
behind Julie's back, reaching up one last time,
for a hug and I had to tell her, had to say, *Julie,
she's trying to hug you* as she desperately tried to hug you to her,
tried to do something, anything as you took your last breath,
your whole body seizing up.
Oh, God, you rasped out and then Julie thanked me for letting her
know what you were trying to do, or, at least, what I think you were
trying to do, and I smiled for the first time in days,
happy you were finally gone because I couldn't stand to see you like
that anymore.

So I wanted you to know I spoke about it
and they looked bored, my pain just another unwanted and
uninteresting thing
as if it were another grammar lesson.

And, strangely, I am grateful for that,
for the not-pretending,
grateful for them slumping in their chairs,
for the eye rolls and glances at the clock.

I guess I really don't know what I'm trying to say here.

I miss you.

It's 10:26 a.m. September 26th, 2013,
and I'm sitting in the library again.
Nothing much has changed.
People are still killing each other all over the world.
God still does or doesn't exist.

And the whole place is bursting with beauty.

I love you.

Jamie

53630135R00035

Made in the USA
Charleston, SC
15 March 2016